Stories of Water

ISBN 978-91-987081-2-7
Stories of Water All rights reserved
Spirit Road ⌒ Bastad Sweden 2021

STORIES OF WATER

Stories written by: Michael V. Coles, Hazel McDonald, Maryana Kolesnik, Carole Bubar-Blodgett, Katie Rutledge, Ash Miner, Franseska Anette Mortensen, Janey Verney, Carina Johansson, Angelique Rodriguez, Magnus Pamp, Lina Petersdotter Johansson, Marie Bech, Dorianne Daniels, Camilla Hjortdal Sindahl, Anna-Katariina Hollmérus, Anna-Carin Martensson

Illustrations and photos by: Maria Yuganova, Lone Aabrink, Franseska Anette Mortensen, Modesty Sofronenkoff, Carina Johansson, Dorianne Daniels, Anna-Katariina Hollmerus, Kia Enbarr, Marie Bech, Lina Petersdotter Johansson and Anna-Carin Martensson

THANK YOU!

Thanks to all who have supported this project by proofreading, giving good advice and being supportive and enthusiastic in general!

Zara Waldeback, Jonathan Horwitz, Julia Crabtree, Andy Polson, Maria Ayre, Henrik Martensson, Lala Birchak, John Rutledge, Jen Hoy, Mads Wittrup Laursen, Caroline Laursen, Britta Rohlén and Leslie Davis.

Michael V. Coles, Vancouver, B.C. Canada

A Mothers Son

When I was young, my mother taught me to give thanks to the water.

Mother also told me that:

Whenever you are sad, or crying, that I should drink a glass of water.

When I ask why, she explained it like this:

Son, there is love in the water for you, that will make you happy again.

How does she know this, I asked?

I know this, for I am the one who put it there for you.

I put it there so you can feel my love when you drink it,

And when you do, you will feel right as rain again.

So, drink a glass of love and give thanks every day!

Hazel McDonald, Ontario, Canada

photo by Modesty Sofronenkoff

The Story of Water

As long as I can remember I have appreciated water.

I was a small girl and I can still recall the exact spot I understood it was precious. I was in tall grass in a field. I had this thought.. "don't waste it". I am one of those who look and ponder bugs, trees, creatures and all the elements.

I played constantly on the Sydenham river bank in Dresden, Ontario, Canada. It was our playground.

I was blessed to spend lots of time the early years visiting on a native reserve, Walpole Island, where my aunt had a tiny cottage on a leased plot, facing the big blue river St Clair.

I live near Lake Erie. Although I never knew him, my grandfather was a great lakes commercial fisherman.

Water calls me, it always has. And I always knew water was powerful. For me, it was intuitive and innate.

Even in the very gentle movements of water, I knew she was whispering, and could rage, and if you were not careful, take your life. She is the most sacred beautiful being, showing her presence in all her forms, magnifying her essence in our bodies, our breath and all of the universe.

One day, I was at my piano. I looked out and saw an indigenous woman carrying a copper vessel and walking. I had no idea of water walkers. She was alone in this walk with a truck moving behind her. I dashed out with a scribbled note and gave it to the driver. In time by the grace of the Creator, I learned about the sacredness of that water walk, and about the significance of that woman's activity.

Grandmother Josephine and her dedication to water, and her water walks became a turning point. Although I did not know her, I did meet her at a very sacred, intentional ceremony that changed my life.

Water is not a commodity. She is alive and listens. She is sacred. You cannot lie to water. She demands respect. And proactive involvement to protect her.

Later, I was sitting in a djembe class. We were freestyling. Suddenly I had this thought. "You need to hold a world water day ceremony", "you have to declare it". It was as if someone spoke it. We finished drumming. I immediately turned to my friend and said I'm going to hold a world water day gathering. "When?"... "next week".

There, I had declared it. She agreed to help.

I raced out to my car, told my husband. It was a flurry of activity to get the community invited and prepare for it.

Exactly one week later we had indigenous elders bless the water. 60 people attended. We gathered water from many sources. Also, some people brought water. I prepared and planned from some deep place inside me, and a sense of Presence.

The ceremony concluded with a feast, remembering to feast the ancestors. The next morning we took the collective water and repatriated it to the lake, drumming and giving thanks.

I am humbled by the generosity of the indigenous leadership whom I respect, for their inclusion and guidance, and importantly, the encouragement to proceed in what is a call for all humanity, respecting the ways that are only for their culture and what is universal to each of us as global peoples with our own expressions.

Water will heal us and keep us healthy if we start by respecting she is life and sustains us.

Water is music to the soul, hugging our thirst for that connection to the great mystery and the universe.

Thank you for the opportunity to share a little of my story about water. There is just so much more.

Maryana Kolesnick, Russia

Вода

Сказка о девочке и ручейке

О, вода, вода, вода!

Ты – прекрасная всегда,

Двери ты нам открываешь,

Мудрость, силу проявляешь.

Информацию даешь, кажется, что это дождь.

Ты границы проявляешь, берега обозначаешь,

Море, речка, океан, утренний густой туман.

Ты живешь во всех мирах, в деревнях и городах,

Ты снаружи и внутри, ты стихия – посмотри!

Ты приносишь очищенье, ты в словах журчишь – реченье,

Эта дева говорит, словно реченька звучит.

Растворяешь ты болезни, исцеляешь ты поток,

Есть в тебе всегда исток,

Ты горишь и ты мерцаешь, силу нашу проявляешь,

Ты – Великая вода, говоришь с нами всегда.

Water

a tale of a girl and a stream

Oh, water, water, water!

You're always beautiful,

You open doors for us,

Wisdom, strength, you show us.

You give information, it seems like rain.

You manifest the boundaries, You mark the shores,

The sea, the river, the ocean, the thick fog of the morning.

You live in all worlds, in villages and cities,

You're outside and inside, you're the elements – look!

You bring cleansing, you murmur in words – speech,

This maiden speaks like a river sounds.

You dissolve disease, you heal the stream,

There is always a source in you,

You burn and you glimmer, You manifest our power,

You are the Great Water, You speak to us always.

One early foggy summer morning the girl woke up. The first rays of the Sun glided over her pillow. The sun bunnies said to the girl, "It's time, get up, a new day has come, we want to play with you".

The girl stretched herself sweetly, sat up on the bed, and saw that her grandmother was still asleep, and it was still very early. Then the girl pulled on her dress, put her feet into her sandals, and quietly slipped out into the yard. It was early morning, the fog had just gone into the distant fields.

The girl walked down the path to the stream that flowed near their house. The tall grass touched the girl's bare feet, cold droplets of water ran down her shins, her sandals soaked. The birds sang, heralding to the world the beginning of a new day, the wind played with the leaves of the trees, the girl's hair. The sun smiled and warmed the little traveller.

In a few minutes the girl was already at the stream, there was her place of strength. The girl leaned into the stream, took the water in her palms, washed her face and laughed. Cold droplets ran down her face, into her mouth. The water was cool, fresh, clean, she was happy to meet the girl. The girl started splashing water droplets, dancing, and it seemed that the universe itself was dancing with the little girl. Everything around was filled with happiness and joy.

The little girl sat down next to the brook and asked it to tell her about something unusual and distant, for the girl was only 6 years old. Most of which she had lived with her grandmother in the village and had never left the village for somewhere far away. And the brook began to babble, telling of the underworld in which it originated, of treasures and dwarves and trolls and fairies. The girl sat nearby, listening to the babbling of the brook, and imagined a magical world of fairy creatures and treasures.

Suddenly, all of a sudden, a big bird sat on a tree on the other side of the brook, and shrilled. The girl woke up and felt that it was already a long time, and her grandmother, most likely, had already woken up, prepared breakfast and was waiting for her granddaughter. The girl thanked the bird that reminded her that it was time to go back, thanked the brook, promising to come back early tomorrow morning for the next story – and rushed home. She ran through the wet grass and the wind played with her hair, tossing it back. A magical fairy tale lived in the girl´s heart, and a summer sunny day lay ahead.

Carole Bubar-Blodgett, Washington

illustration by Anna-Carin Martensson

Gifts and Insights from the Water is Life Walk 2011

Shared as gifted by spirit Carole Bubar-Blodgett

Water has intelligence, Water is alive, Water has memory. Water transfers emotions received from the vibrations of spoken, written or musical words. Water speaks with the language of energy and responds to the energies of your intentions as well as spoken words.

In 2004 there was a gathering in Hopi Land where Hopi Elder Jerry Honawa shared the truth that "Water has Intelligence".

At the Veterans Centre in Black Mesa, the main speakers were Vernon Masayesva, executive director of Black Mesa Trust, spoke revealing the traditional knowledge of water.

Researcher Dr. Masaru Emoto, chief of the Hado Institute in Tokyo, shared the scientific evidence of the intelligence of water.

Masayesva presented the Hisot Navoti (knowledge of ancestors) while Dr Emoto's film footage showed the actual transformation of water crystals as they were exposed to music and written words. Dr. Emoto's photos demonstrate the changes that occur in water crystals in reaction to human actions, to positive and negative words.

A photo of water crystals that were exposed to the word "peace" flowered into beautiful crystals, while the water crystals that developed in the water exposed to the word "war" were dark and ugly. His photos show, for those who must see to believe, the truth of Traditional Ecological Knowledge (TEK). Water responds to words; both spoken and written. Echoing the words of the elders, who taught me: "your words have the power to heal or hurt, use them wisely".

Masayesva shared Hopi history, "According to the Hopi, long ago there was nothing but water from the beginning of time". This is what we call the First World of Hopi.

The First World was full of harmony, balance, and peace. Hopi still carry water in a gourd recognizing it as a limited resource.

The waters, rivers, lakes, springs, aquifers, glaciers, and oceans all work together in a harmonious exchange to sustain all life.

Hopi have taught me that the aquifers and springs are the Earth Mother's breathing holes. They breathe in snow and rain and breathe it out again.

Human Beings participate in life of water; our prayers and thoughts influence weather bringing in the snow and rain. Masayesva said the people are the trusted guardians of the water and land and... we are not doing our part.

From my experience on the Water is Life Walk I know that the water responded to the vibrations carried in my songs, verbal prayers, and the loving thoughts of water. Water carried that response with it and shared it with everything that it touched. I know this because of the response from the plant and animal nations along the walk.

One example of these reactions came from four cedar trees along the side of Paradise Road coming down off Ti´Swaq (Mt. Rainier).

I stopped to pray at a small stream and noticed these four cedar trees along the edge of the stream. My thoughts went to the Brian M Frisina family and the memory of Teckla and Natani teaching me the song "Cedar Tree".

I began to focus my thoughts on how the water feeds the cedar trees. Then I decided to sing the "Cedar Tree" song in remembrance of the support the Frisina family provided me for the Water is Life Walk. I sang "Cedar Tree" with fond memories of the times spent with this wonderful family and the picture of the joyous little faces teaching me to sing "Cedar Tree". The water carried the vibrations of my feelings, thoughts, and words to the cedar trees. The branches of the cedar tree closest to me began to sway slightly; just a few branches at first then more joined until the whole tree swayed gently. I looked around to see if there was a breeze but nothing else was moving!

As I thanked the water for carrying thoughts and emotions expressed in the words of the song the other three cedar trees joined in the dance of gratitude.

As I have thought back and focused on this moment, I have realized that water is in everything. My Breath of Life contains the Sacred Water that remembered and shared my thoughts, feelings and emotions with the water in the air; the water in the air remembered and shared them with the water in the cedar tree.

My body is 75% water (60%-98% depending on method used when measuring) and it heard and remembered my thoughts, feelings, and emotions; the water in my body shared them with the water within the soil and it passed it on to the plants, trees, stone people, the birds and animals.

Everything that touched or drank the water received the vibrations created by this prayer for the Water of Life!

Later a mole, that lives below ground, would come above ground and cross the pavement just after the high noon prayer to let me know I was heard. The goose gifted feathers all along the walk; at every body of water I blessed, feathers where left. The deer, the raven, the chipmunk, and many others went out of their way, to make their presence known, and gave thanks for blessing the Water of Life.

Water, the Chief of the Elements and the Ultimate Healer

The first element we develop a relationship within this world is water. We grow and develop in our mother's womb surrounded by water.

At birth, the water breaks and flows out leading us into this world. Our human bodies are 75% to 85% water. We truly are water babies! We are the water! Water has a collective memory. Our bodies have the information stored in the water that our mothers drank; that we have drunk from the moment of our birth and the water that comprises our bodies at this very moment.

As I have meditated on the power of water to remember and share information, I developed a better understanding of the glass of water at my bedside every night. Since I was old enough to remember my grandmother had us take a big glass of water into our bedroom, we drank half and left the other half and drank it in the morning before getting up.

This became a habit and later in life sitting with an elder as I bedded down for the night, I took my glass of water and drank half then sat the other half on the floor beside my cot. "Who taught you that prayer?" came Uncle's voice from his cot. "What prayer?" … "The water prayer". I explained it was a habit.

He then taught me the prayer that went with that simple ceremony.

Now I understand that water collects and remembers our thoughts and feelings. I understand the aura of my glass of water encircles me as I sleep, collecting and remembering my dreams as I sleep. This knowledge allows me to tap into my dreamtime in a much more powerful way as I say my morning prayer with the glass of water, I ask it to bring forth anything from my dream-time that I need to remember right now. This has become an amazing tool…I tap into memories of dreams from years ago that now have a new lesson to teach.

Water is the ultimate healer and should be your first medicine. Water is the great Peacemaker establishing the first great peace; the peace we must find within ourselves to create peace in the world around us. This is a powerful personal healing available to all of us. Our bodies are 70% to 85% water depending on age, sex and body part; by praying for the water, you drink each day and filling it with love and peace we can fill ourselves with that love and peace. Our mind, body, spirit, and emotions are all connected! As we fill ourselves with positive thoughts and feelings these positive emotional energies affect our mind, spirit and bodies creating an overall increase in health. Water is the source of all life!

As our blood (mostly water) flows through our body it transports oxygen, nutrients, and energies both positive and negative. I have several health issues that have been improved just by asking the water to go to that area of my body and work. I utilize water as a healer both externally and internally.

When I go to the river, lake, or ocean I do a traditional water blessing…dipping under in the four directions; now I have incorporated this blessing when I shower or bathe in the tub. In the shower I step in and out of the water, I find this to be more effective with cold water. Then I warm it up.

Developing a personal relationship (connection) with water will change you in mind and body.

Everything in the universe is made up of energies, or vibrations if that term works better for you. Dr. Emoto calls these energies (vibrations) Hado.

Our words and thoughts carry with them certain vibrations. We can heal ourselves with our thoughts; cancer patients report remissions or shrinking tumors just from focused thought. Hado medicine utilizes these energies and the power of water to transmit these energies throughout the body.

The way whales depend on the water to carry the vibrations created by their songs.

Emotions and illness

There is a close connection between our emotions and illness.

Each emotion that causes DIS-ease in our body has a cancelling emotion:

> ~ Stress can be cancelled by Relaxation
>
> ~ Perplexity can be canceled by Good Grace
>
> ~ Worry can be canceled by Acceptance
>
> ~ Excess Fear can be canceled by Peace of Mind
>
> ~ Irritability can be canceled by Calmness
>
> ~ Anxiety can be canceled by Relief
>
> ~ Anger can be canceled by Compassion
>
> ~ Loneliness can be canceled by Friendship
>
> ~ Apathy can be canceled by Passion
>
> ~ Sadness can be canceled by Joy
>
> ~ Impatience can be canceled by Tolerance
>
> ~ Grudge is cancelled by Gratitude

By praying with the Water of Life and asking the Creator (Father God) to fill the water with the energy of relaxation I can create the vibration of relaxation within my body by simply drinking that water. Water is so generous that the water I drink will share the healing energy with all the water in my body.

WE ARE THE WATER so going to the source of our life first to heal us only makes good sense. This is not new knowledge it is incredibly old knowledge, most of our ancestors went to water twice a day even in the winter. You can write the words love, gratitude, compassion or any one of the healing energies that you need then laminate it and turn it into a coaster. If you use a clear glass the water will absorb the energy of that word. I have made coasters with all of the healing energies listed above. I have used pieces of clear contact paper to laminate coasters to save money. The energy of gratitude and love increases our immunity.

Our words have great power; when you talk to the water envision the positive result that you are praying for. You do not have to be a medicine person to heal yourself! You DO have to have positive feelings and believe that the water is listening and will produce the desired result. Do not expect overnight healing…dis-ease does not develop overnight ~ nor does the healing.

Healing our water will take many people praying all the time for our water. Remember our ancestors each prayed for the Water of Life twice a day every day. These ways have been lost by many and we are just beginning to return to this practice. Imagine the positive change we could make in our water if all prayed for the water where we live!

The Peace Within

Even if we just talk to the water we use for drinking, cooking, bathing, or showering, doing dishes, laundry, watering your plants and garden. If we simply say thank you, I respect you, and I love you we strengthen the water. That water will travel the world and carry that blessing to whatever part of the world it rains down on!

I believe that it is possible to create world peace simply by praying for our Water of Life. If we fill the water, we drink with the Hado of peace (energy of peace) … that water will fill us with peace; when it leaves our body, it will still carry that energy of peace wherever it goes.

Our human bodies are approximately 75% water…so if I am 75% Peace, I will be able to control any emotion that could disrupt that peace.

"The first peace, which is the most important, is that which comes from within the souls of men when they realize their relationship, their oneness, with the Universe and all its powers, and when they realize that at the centre of the Universe dwells Wakan Tanka, and that this centre is really everywhere, it is within each of us. This is the real peace, and the others are but reflections of this.

The second peace is that which is made between two individuals and the third is that which is made between two nations.

But above all you should understand that there can never be peace between nations until there is first known that true peace which is within the souls of man." Black Elk ~ Sacred Pipe

Remember – water is the mirror of our spirit; it reflects our thoughts and feelings. It helps us develop into the human being we choose to be.

Shared as gifted by spirit Carole Bubar-Blodgett

Katie Rutledge, Northern Ireland

photo by Franseska Anette Mortensen

WaterWays

As someone who has lived much of my life upon the island of Ireland, Water is a constant feature in the weather and of general conversation as though somehow it shouldn't be there or it has outstayed its welcome. And yet the Emerald Isle would not be emerald and our neighbourly exchanges would not be the same without it.

Many are the ways of Water and so must the descriptions of Water be.

In the depths of the Waters there is a wink and a smile that stretches from one end of the unending to the other end of the unbeginning. The Fire in the Middle bursts forth from the smooth face of the Waters, roaring and seeking height and solidity while the Waters simply settle and rest, waiting.

Fiercely blow the Solar Winds of Air, cooling, lifting, stroking the face of the Waters and soothing and inciting the raging Fire.

The ground of the Earth cools and brings forth the seed of Creation. Life continues.

The child stirs the stick in the water.

"Where does this water come from?" she asks her mother.

"It bubbles up from below" says her mother as she fills her jar with the clear water.

"Where is below?"

"Down, beneath our feet, deep within the ground."

"Is the water always there?"

"Let us hope so" says the mother and she takes the child's hand and hurries away to the day that is calling her.

A tiny frog perches on the edge of the pond. The grasses tremble and the sunlight disappears. The frog leaps and a huge scything narrowness pierces the air and the water in a continuous movement. Little Frog darts and finds a welcome stone on the bed of the pond under which to shelter. The Heron preens its feathers in a show of patience.

Water is a source of life and a witness to life's endings.

Here is a story about the Moon and Water.

Moon reaches out to the Waters on the Earth to have the experience of what she once knew. In return she powers the Waters through lines of energy anchored at special node points in the oceans, in the subterranean caverns and in the blind water springs that curl below the Earth's surface extruding power and possibility.

When the Moon sings her beautiful filigreed songs, the Moon Lines quiver and hum with the vibration of silver light and the Water is tempted and yearns to reconnect with the Moon. Who knows? The Night may come.

I re-member my parts in my journey of healing, walking towards the wholeness that I am. Who is the memory of Water, the re-membering of the reservoir of emotions and how am I to help Water to re-member, to regain wholeness?

She offers me, if I can think of the Ocean as She, a twisted stick on the beach, a fine water wand to wield with love and care in the flowing waters of a stream or a creek or a brook or a river. I hold the tip of the wand in the gossiping or serious water and ask for healing to flow through the Water Cycle, from this place to the sea and from there to the clouds and from there to the raindrops cascading down upon the Earth's face to enter the quiet or noisy watercourse, intent on flowing and completing this circuitous route.

One voice, but with intent. One voice, but not so. Here are many others – loving, caring, helping, vivifying. Pure intention to bring purity to Water. Pure Water to bring purity to Life. We gather in circle to encircle Water with our love as Water encircles the Planet and brings life.

Water Haiku

Love in Waters Pure

Unbeginning unending

May you always be.

illustration by Anna-Carin Martensson

The Meeting of Waters

The Element of Water had called the monthly full moon meeting of all the waters on Gaia. There would be another at the new moon. During these very important gatherings, all the waters determined their human ranking by color. The older waters were gathering pollution, and often had to change their status. New waters, especially in early spring after rains in areas riddled with drought, needed to learn their designation in the world. Younger waters often had a bit of trouble with their assignments, so special care and time was always taken to explain the workings of the world to them.

Naturally, the great Oceans arrived first. So vast and all-encompassing, they had the least travel to do. The Lakes arrived next, large and powerful bodies of fresh water.

Followed by Rivers, fast flowing and full, they arrived with a whoosh, and everyone could hear them coming well in advance. Ponds came next, the complete opposite, so still and calm, but just as large in volume. Creeks came after Ponds, followed shortly by Streams.

Creeks and Streams, narrower and not quite as powerful as Rivers, but just as swift in some places. Springs that came up out of the ground were a little late, because they had lost track of time without the sun and moon. Puddles came last, and all sizes of Puddles were welcome. Waterfalls, Rain, Hurricane, Tidal Wave, Ice, Snow, and Tide, each had a representative to stay in the loop.

When all the Waters of Gaia had arrived and taken their place in the great Circle of Waters, the Element of Water spoke, "Welcome, Waters of Gaia, to our Circle! To the old Waters, thank you for sharing your patience, wisdom, and generosity with us as we initiate the new Waters. As you all know, humans have color-coded us into the following categories: shallow or bright blue, deep or dark blue, drinkable or fresh and clear, dirty or brown, algae or green, oily or black and iridescent, and polluted or gunky."

Eagerly, a new Creek raised her hand. When called on by the Element of Water she said, "Excuse me, I have a question. Isn't all water clear? Why do humans give us color designations? We are all one Water."

The Element of Water smiled, patiently. This happened at every meeting. "Humans have all different colors, so that's how they relate to each other and the world around them." The Element of Water said, wisely, "We try to help them enjoy and take care of us by following their labels."

The new Creek simply looked puzzled, but didn't raise her hand again. This didn't make sense yet. She decided to wait and see if more listening would do the trick. She listened intently.

"Now, Oceans, would any of you like to change your status from Dark Blue?" The Element of Water asked, curiously.

The Atlantic Ocean raised its hand, "I need to change from my usual dark blue to gunky. There is a lot of plastic pollution circulating in my currents, and I'm afraid that takes up more of my surface than ever before."

The Element of Water scribbled furiously in her notebook, and without looking up said, "Thank you, Atlantic. I concur with your assessment, and your request is approved."

A young, but not new Creek raised his hand, "Since Atlantic isn't dark blue anymore, can I be dark blue now? I don't want to be brown anymore. Dark blue attracts a lot more people and boats and all sorts of fun things!"

The Element of Water looked at the young Creek sternly, and said with absolute authority, "Creek, we talked about this at your first meeting, but I'll go over it again for all the New Waters. There is NO WAY a Creek, Stream, Pond, Puddle, or River can ever be deep enough to be considered dark blue. Dark blue is reserved exclusively for Lakes and Oceans. That's just the way it is. Trying to falsely label yourself as another Water's color will not be tolerated."

The young Creek looked down, a little disappointed, "Oh, yes, Element of Water, I remember now. Thank you, and sorry for interrupting." It was worth a try.

The Element of Water continued the meeting, "Would anyone else like to change their designation before we make assignments for all the new Waters?"

Silence fell. It seemed Atlantic was the only Water with an update for this meeting.

"Okay, great! Please step forward, new Waters!" The Element of Water said eagerly, with a warm smile.

All the new Waters, from Puddles to Streams, stepped forward. The Element of Water explained how assignments would be given.

"Welcome, new Waters! When receiving your assignments, we base our decision on the Land where you live."

Whispers and confusion sprung up. The new Waters didn't understand how something they had no control over, the spot in the Land they were born into, determined their classification.

"Yes, yes. The Land is what determines your assignment. I know it's not fair, because Rain just drops you somewhere that is not necessarily your preference, but it's a fact of life on Gaia with humans. If Rain drops you on dirt or sand, those are both brown substances, so you will be brown Puddles, Ponds, Creeks, Streams, and Rivers. Generally, only Waters on Stone are considered clear. Shallow Waters on white sand with no mud are usually light blue, and Lakes or Oceans that reach a depth of 100 feet or more are considered dark blue. Now Rivers that are moving so fast over rocks they have white caps on their waves are called White Waters, that's the only exception. Does anyone have any questions?"

One of the new Puddles raised her hand, "Excuse me. I'm a tiny little puddle on a road made of asphalt. What color am I?"

"Thank you for asking, Puddle" The Element of water nodded, patiently, "Your assignment is black."

The new Puddle looked completely repulsed for a moment, "Okay, thank you" was the most polite response she could come up with. What a lonely assignment, being stuck on a human road, not even on a natural piece of Land.

The Element of Water had ensured all the new Waters had their assignments. To finish up the meeting, the Element of Water wanted to make sure everyone knew what was coming,

"As most of us are aware, climate change is resulting in a lot more melting of ice at the poles of Gaia, but also warming up the lands and leading to a lot more evaporation and drought. It is highly likely that some of you smaller Waters, Puddles, Ponds, and Creeks will not be at the next meeting. Please don't worry, most likely you will eventually become Rain, or you'll be nourishment for vitally important Plants, Animals, or Fungi. No one is unimportant, just because they won't be here for very long. All Waters on Gaia are treasured by all other beings. So, until the next meeting, please flow peacefully and powerfully with life."

All the Waters bowed respectfully and gratefully to the Element of Water. One by one, they returned to their places on Gaia.

When it was just the Element of Water left and she was all alone, her smile faded. Concern and sadness came across her face. She knew her children weren't being taken care of by humans as well as they could be. She knew she was being taken for granted.

Suddenly, a sweet song of thanksgiving met the Element of Water's ears. There were still some humans who treasured her as she deserved. A soft grin came, she closed her eyes and listened to the prayers of these beautiful people. The expression on her face was pure bliss. Their heartfelt gratitude brought her joy.

"Yes," she thought, "there is still hope. I must get back to work".

Franseska Anette Mortensen, Denmark

Water is my element

The sky is turning brighter. Just slightly and very gradually. Long before the sun rises, the grey and black darkness slowly dissolves into all nuances of blue. First they seem weak as if mixed up with coal, with ashes, with the pelage of the black cat from my childhood; the colours emerge at snail speed. The blushing of the East adds warmth into the blue and starts to create what we are hoping for every day, longing for every day, living for every day. A new day.

And I'm out. Out, running all the way to the beach to see if the water is still there. Out, running the pavements and the paths of the suburb that all of a sudden has become the enclave of nature I always dreamt it would be. Birds on repeat trying to drown out each other's song. The blackbird warning of cats, the rooster proclaiming that day is coming, the sparrow, the dove, the magpie, the wren, the greenfinch – all are communicating.

And as I don't know their languages it all is music to me. I imagine they are saluting the new day, the new energy, the new life once again, just like they did yesterday. A hare is crossing the path near the empty playground, a squirrel in a tree sees me, the grass sees me, the leaves on the birch want to have a look around – they're on the verge of blooming with the tree stretching its branches to catch the first rays of the morning sun, shortly to be seen.

But still it is invisible. The star we call the sun. It has been notifying of its coming, but still no one will spot it in my part of the world, the East of Jutland, Denmark. Long before we watch it rising, the colours of our surroundings are awakened by it as it spreads its rays far around by constantly throwing fire into the universe. Reportedly we see the first glowing edge of the sun a couple of minutes before we actually should be able to do so, before it has actually lifted itself high enough to reach the edge of the globe seen from our point of view. The refraction of light wants to spread joy already before the sun tips over the rim. Before the solar disk, the ultimate circular, slowly but still too fast, is lifting itself into our realm. Glowing white behind its purple robe, changing colour every second until it undresses before us, shining too bright to let us look at it.

We believe in what we see and what we experience. We believe that the Sun rises even though we know that it is we that move, it is the globe called Earth with all its blue oceans that is circling in orbit around the sun and rotates around itself at the same time. All of it so far beyond what we can fathom that it only makes sense to say: The sun is rising.

One day floating in the bay, staring at the sunrise, I shouted out my joy "Hooray, the Earth is turning!" It didn't sound right. Shouting "Hooray, the Sun is rising!" always sounds better and is always true because it marks the magical moment. And because that's what we experience, it is empirically true that the sun rises.

Seen from a point just above our navels the Earth doesn't move, it's the sun that moves. Deep inside we agree with Ptolemy claiming his geocentric model of the world: The Earth is in the middle like we are all are the main characters of each our own lives. Standing with both our feet firmly planted on the ground we only move when we want to.

The Sun moves so that in summer it rises above the North of Risskov but in winter it rises above Mols – all seen from the place on the beach, in the bay of Aarhus that is mine, and where we'll soon be arriving. In an instant I'll reach that place, running paths and pavement, running dew and grass, with my feet lifted and in brief fractions of seconds at a time levitating over the eternally rotating Earth, landing always in a new spot. The Sun is setting its course, following its path, then finally setting on the far side of Jutland, sinking into the waves of the North Sea. And behind the nearest house blocks seen from my personal epicentre.

The place I call mine and which I wholeheartedly share with everyone else believing it is also theirs: The beach, the bathing jetty, the water. First and foremost: The water. The huge pool with space enough for everyone who wants to enter. It is calling me, even louder than the Sun and the loudest when they are collaborating. The first two, the beach and the jetty are quickly done with. Clothes removed in a hurry, running shoes forget they have shoelaces and jump off my feet. The water is alluring. From the moment I wake up knowing it probably still exists, I hear it calling, tempting me. And its call gets seven miles stronger when I catch the first glimpse of the bay. My inner gramophone plays the sounds of roaring Pacific waves hitting the coast of South America and the surge of the waves hitting the boat last summer in Limfjorden. It plays the ripple of the brook, the clinking of ice broken by the wind at Tjele Langsø and it even plays the water of the tap running to amuse the cats of my present life.

The Sun is calling, the water is calling and once again I got there in time. No matter what kind of watery tones are ringing in my inner ears, the happiness is greatest when accompanied by the Sun on its initial journey.

When the day is dawning, when the sun is rising ever so fast to make it through the day. In these moments everything fits. I live for the minutes bathing in a sea of colours, swimming in blue, red, orange nuances I couldn't possibly capture with my camera though I keep trying. I live for these moments as I live for my daughters – and my cats. As I live for everything and everyone that enriches my life and brings me the happiness I keep seeking for.

I swim towards the rising Sun. I face the Sun at dawn looking at it, looking at the water, observing the golden stripe of small suns constantly floating and moving in front of me like a tadpole,

the reversed tail of a comet, a sea iguana making its way through the water. I steer towards the Sun as if it were approachable, as if I could keep on swimming, as if every stroke with my hands in the water would bring me just one light-second closer to the Sun. I bathe in the sea of the Sun, united with the sunbeams and the water. The human body contains approximately sixty percent water but here we are one. As if I dilute, dissolve and disappear, become insignificant; and at the same time the Sun, the water and I are all that exist in this world.

In these moments I experience the greatest freedom, the greatest happiness and joy, the greatest connection with all there is. The entire surface of my naked body is in contact with the water. Small bubbles of air on my thighs and my back keeps my body a bit warmer for a short while but soon they will be blown away meeting water molecules and harsh waves and as a result of my strokes in the water, my swimming in the sunny sea. The water embraces me, nourishes me, caresses me.

I swim in the stripe of sun that is mine in this moment, situated right in front of me. On the bathing jetty stands a friend. Her skinny dip was briefer than mine. She dries her body with a towel, puts on her clothes and just stands there.

She is. She also has a stripe of sun right in front of her and watches it glitter; she closes her eyes, still seeing what she just saw.

A glimpse of warmth from the Sun hits her eyelids and warms her soul; just what she needed in that moment. Also he who entered the water straight from the beach has his stripe of sun. In fact everyone standing near water facing the Sun has a stripe of sun right in front of them. There are sunny stripes for all of us. We could all be united around the globe, along the water's edge looking at each of our sunny stripes. Together. All over this globe we call the Earth, in places where it's daytime and clouds let us. We can feel each other if we want. Touch each other's hearts if we dare. Watching the Sun in the water. And feeling it inside of us.

We are several who on a daily basis have a skinny dip at this place that is both mine and everyone else's. Many of us are very talkative but sometimes a silence strikes us – an utter silence conquers the space.

All we hear is the crying of the seagulls, the surge of the waves, the weak rattling of clothes being taken on or off.

Not a word is spoken.

A silent presence connects us better than all those words we often throw out without thinking what the consequences of breaking the silence are. Now we swim, we lie still in the water, stand in the water, tread water; present in the moment. The silence in the water makes us able to listen to what it might tell us. We stop ourselves from falling into the trap of small talk. A smile and a glance at the sun also connects us. We shut off the auto pilot, the always chattering old women and the sometimes a bit grumpy old men are silent; we stop disturbing ourselves and each other. We reset ourselves, more able to see, now listening to our inner voices and not just what tumbles out of our mouths. Breathing with the water, holding our hands above the water like in a silent prayer and to keep our fingers from getting too cold.

At other times we unite in laughter. Laughing at waves who want to topple us and throw us around in explosions of water.

Laughing at water striking up through the cracks between the boards of the jetty, the wind that demands the life of a sock or two, feeding it to the sea. Laughing at a shoe slipping into the water and me entering the sea again to catch it before it floats away, resulting in me having to run back home with one foot wet. Laughing at those who shriek as they enter the cold water, feeling the thrill and laughing at themselves too.

Jumping for joy on those days when the waves make us do so. Laughter and life, and the swirl of the foamy crest of the waves.

Sometimes the sea disappears. Abducted by the mist the horizon dissolves, everything turns white. Invisible clouds of water molecules conquer other water molecules. Above and beneath. Mist, rain, snow and hail. But it is always there, the sea, the bay, the water; and we prove it every day by entering it, swimming in it, shivering and gasping if that's how it is for you.

Every day I take photos in the water. Of the water, the Sun, people and birds in the water, silhouettes of kayaks several light-minutes away as they almost make it to the sun, hitting it in a split second before they paddle on. I am a photographer and I accidently bought a small waterproof camera a few years ago having just gone away for the summer holidays, with the decision to take a break from photography while away. But also having totally forgotten that I had ordered that small waterproof camera to be delivered at my holiday address.

That ruined the plan. But a brand new world opened itself to me. The water I knew, photography I knew, but the combination was explosive.

The holiday took place near the third deepest lake in Denmark, thirty one metres deep at the most. Where I usually swim there's a pontoon and entering the water from its ladder, it's already nine metres deep. I keep myself pretty near the surface, only my toes sometimes reach some one and a half metres deep and the camera even less. Catching small fish, bathers, raindrops striking the surface, glittering waves, the sun rays beaming through the water hitting my body creating unpredictable patterns. Lots of small bubbles of air, dirt and life. Playing with the camera tightly fastened around my wrist. Taking long swims in the lukewarm water with my new best friend.

We look so beautiful below the water. Everything turns soft and round due to the altered light qualities. Breasts take revenge over the heavy yoke of gravity and all women become twenty something again. All men twenty something plus one. The water makes us young and alive, light as fairies, as butterflies. We are fish in the water, birds in the air, crabs in the sand. We are in our element. So obvious.

It is this little waterproof camera I bring for my daily swim. It is this camera that has made me swim so far in my longing to reach the Sun, this camera that has taught me to stay for so long in the cold water that I completely forget about temperatures in order to get the right photo.

Deeply concentrated with focus on nothing else other than creating the best possible picture out of the physical appearance of the elements. It may take minutes, sometimes several. And after those minutes my body has merged with the water and the water stopped being cold.

It just kind of doesn't have any temperature at all, it's just water and pure presence in that moment. And I don't want to leave it,

I don't want to get up and get dressed, I could stay in there like forever it seems. Wellness in the natural way. It is only my common sense that makes me do what I must: Get up, get dressed, get warm. My body and my soul don't want to leave, I'm totally in love with the water and the feeling it gives me. To me it is quite normal at this time of year when the calendar says spring but the weather still votes for winter, that I stay in the water for six to ten minutes, maybe sometimes more. I have no idea, I just am and only my photos can tell me if I let them.

And in winter when the water is below zero but still doesn't freeze because of the salt, maybe less. In the slush ice when I practice my skills of being an ice cube surrounded by nature's own natural ice cubes. In summer of course much longer, taking long swims towards the Sun along the shore.

I sometimes get the strange thought that I and some of my bathing companions around the world may carry remnants from ancient times when the reptile-bird-fish hadn't yet quite left the huge oceans, hadn't yet quite decided to live on land. I don't want to leave when I'm there. It is mine. Water is my element.

But it hasn't always been like that. The pleasure of skinny dipping into the cold water of the Danish winter I had known for many years. Always a little scared if I hadn't been there for a while. My brain and my body unable to remember the pleasure but longing for the heat of the sauna after the dip. Dripping sweat and salty water onto the towels. Gasping for my breath when I entered the cold water again after the sauna.

That was then. Now is now and completely different. Only the cold water remains and lots of it. Two years ago I discovered the bathing jetty at the beach close enough to my flat for me to put on my running shoes and run there. Close enough to even run back afterwards, sometimes looking a bit like an arthritis patient with stiff muscles and joints like an old soup hen hardly worth slaughtering; windswept and getting even colder by the chill factor hitting me uphill after the swim.

The jetty became mine. There are many who would state they are in a relationship with the bathing jetty if face book would let them. Both women and men. Mostly women though. We're in an almost erotic relationship with the water, always longing for its embrace. We take off our clothes and dive into its arms, completely naked.

Even in summer we swim naked early in the morning before all the families with their small kids arrive and kind of plant themselves on the beach with towels, bikinis and soft drinks. Roots in the sand, eyes facing the sunglasses. And not even in winter do I miss the sauna. I can live all day and sometimes even the next on the boost of energy I get from the cold water's embrace. I don't want to erase that feeling with the heat of a sauna. Seven minutes and you're reborn, reset, ready.

I face the sun at dawn even when it's not there. Because it always is, even when we cannot see it. One thing is for sure, it rises every morning yet still we experience every new day as a miracle, a new hope, a new beginning. We take nothing for granted, not even what probably is. Rediscovering makes us happy.

The next day it fills me up again. Gives me an energy and joy that makes me more able to cope with whatever happens in life. To be more kind. The water embraces me and teaches me. The water will remember me and I the water. We bond.

My body is connected to the water. And through the water connected to the shore on the other side of the bay. To the luminous yellow hills and the horses grassing far from the paths, to every little bird at the sides of and flying over Stubbe Sø, to every beetle and every fly on a carcass. To all living and all that must die. My naked body has no boundaries, my skin is open and connected. We are one; the Sun and the water, me and all of us. All there is. We gladly drift out with the tide to rescue shipwrecked mermaids, entangled octopuses, fish that have swallowed too much sea water.

Today the sun rose at two minutes to half past six. No, in reality it was two minutes to half past five, but someone has changed the time. I was there. Silver linings shone like gold when I descended the stairs and plunged into the water of the bay.

Water and sunrise. It doesn't get any bigger. And it never becomes a cliché even though both you and I have seen it a thousand times before. A kiss never becomes a cliché, a hug doesn't either. All that nourishes us endures a thousand repetitions and more.

This morning the sea hugged me for about six minutes. My skin got cold, my arms felt like they were not really mine. But my heart got warm. The sun rose right there before me. Above the water, in the water.

Janey Verney, Wales

Ayodya 1979

first time in another continent

so far from home

three parched travellers sprawled out flat

on a bed in a concrete room

drained by sun and dust

abandoned to heavy heat

with shock of sudden sound

the showerhead sprays to life

instant energy

craving bodies rush

under the flow

joyful screaming

splashing

with new understanding why

people

worship

water

Wales 2021

i am water

here on my spacious surface

are treetops

the sky

and gently falling rain

which you have not yet felt

drops line up below a branch

waiting to fall

to trigger

expanding maps

where water plants sit still

a stone building undulates

and two birds fly through this other place

at the edge

my overflowing power

changes direction

suddenly

do not assume you know where I will go

Carina Johansson, Sweden

illustration by Carina Johansson

The Woman and the Dragonfly

Once upon a time. Yes, because that is the place where this story begins.

Once upon a time there was a young girl who was severely afraid of Water, although she loved playing with the ocean waves just at the edge of the breaking point at the shore. Even though she found it very funny and exciting to put her little boats of bark, sticks and leaves in the creeks and rivers and watch them being carried away by the flowing streams, she herself did not dare to go into these sources of Water.

She did not dare to go into any source of deep and flowing Water.

She deeply longed to, but she was absolutely sure that if she did she would immediately be pulled down and drown.

As a child she never learned to swim because of this fear. In school she refused to go into the Water during swimming classes which made her teacher furious.

However, she did not trust that this angry woman was the one to keep her safe in the Water. She did not trust her own capability to swim and float either and she certainly did not trust Water to carry her.

Years later she still carried the wish to be able to swim within her heart. Not because she was forced to by anyone but because of her deep, deep love for Water and for her longing to be with Water without fear.

One midsummer day she sat by a quiet forest lake among the pine trees. As she sat there, she felt this strange pull to go into the Water. Somewhere inside of her an ancient memory began to take form and float up to the surface of her mind and she felt that she somehow belonged to the Water, was a part of Water and that Water was a part of her. At her very first arrival to this earth walk she had peacefully rested inside her mother's womb surrounded by Water and she remembered this peace.

So, she rose up and stepped into the lake, the Water was cold and fresh as it embraced her ankles. She stepped out deeper and deeper and as the Water touched her belly, fear began to rise within her. Then a shimmering blue Dragonfly appeared. Hoovering in front of her eyes, she admired its beauty and as it began flying around her, she felt safe and she remembered her connection with Water once again.

The Dragonfly flew in front of her in a joyous dance and step by step she walked further out into the lake until the Water finally reached over the top of her head.

That evening she stayed in the lake for a very long time.

She learned how to swim as the dogs do, she learned how to swim as the turtles do, she learned how to float on her back and let the Water carry her, embrace her and she felt at one with Water. She felt joy. She felt at home.

From that day on, no longer did she fear Water. From that day on, no longer did she fear Life.

By now the girl has turned into a woman with silver in her hair. Many years have passed since the time when she was afraid of Water and Water itself has brought her many teachings along the way.

Water that is the amazing living organism that is a part of each cell within her human body. Water that is all around her.

This Water that she shares with every living being upon the Earth.

Water that is the source of Life.

Anna-Carin Martensson, Sweden

illustrations by Anna-Carin Martensson

The Story of Water

Once upon a time there was a little girl who loved to walk around in Nature. She was used to do that because she lived in the countryside with her family and had been following her grandfather on his daily walks ever since she was a toddler. They often walked down to the stream and on this particular day she was walking a little bit ahead.

She stepped in to the shallow creek. Mmm, she just loved the feel of the cold water as it flowed around her feet. A little song came and the girl joined in the melody as she stood in the stream.

She was in a particularly sweet and loving mood that day and was thinking about all the joy she felt when she was playing with water or going for a swim and about how good a glass of cold water was when she was thirsty. She thought about this and all the good things that Water had done for her all of her life.

Her heart was full of gratitude and suddenly she said, "Dear Water, what can I do for you?" The girl was not really expecting an answer but almost immediately the answer came, "You can help by telling my story!" The girl was so surprised that she missed what Water said next but after a moment of puzzlement she heard:

"…at this point in the Creation I was everywhere. Everything was moving – it still is – the Stars were singing the most beautiful songs and I loved nothing more than to flow around and listen to them."

"– I heard music that I had never heard before. My attention was drawn to it at once and the rest of me followed.

I saw that the Angels and a lot of other amazing energies had gathered with the Stars to sing a Song of Creation and it was fantastic!"

"Together they sang Gaia into life!"

48

"When she was born and let out her first cry which echoed throughout space, I could not help falling in love with her.

But it was even more than that, I heard a note in that song that made me surrender completely.

The note was me, so totally in harmony with my inner being that I was compelled to manifest into form."

"So that is how I came to Earth, as you call her. To me she will always be Gaia and I love her! I will always love her and I will, for as long as I am able, cool her with my swirling waters where she needs it. I clean the air for her and help her to move all manner of things that have ended up in the wrong place. I sing and dance with joy to make her happy and try to hold my note in harmony with her singing. You know, it is the song that does it!"

"Does it?" asked the girl.

"The song amplifies the life force by its vibrations of joy and love!" Water explained.

"Lately it has become harder to hear her. So many things are out of tune that it is hard for me to hear her song through all the disharmonies. Would you be able to tell your friends that it would be a good thing for us all if we could help her sing?"

The little girl's eyes were filled with tears as she had listened deeply and felt so many things – the beauty of all the Angels and energies singing the song of Creation, the love that Water felt for Gaia. She felt fear and sadness too as she thought of all the people living on earth and understanding so little about life – all of them, all of humanity out of tune!

"Of course, I want to help by singing the song," said the little girl, "but I can't hear it at all and in any case, I am not good at singing! So even though what you are asking might sound simple, to me it is impossible!"

"That was the answer I thought you would give," said Water, "because you humans are all trapped in your minds – but not every problem can be solved by thinking about it!"

"It is my love for Gaia that keeps me in this form, that keeps my rivers flowing and the waves of my oceans rocking in rhythm with the beat of her heart.

What you need to do is go out and look and feel and smell and let yourself be enchanted by her beauty. Let yourself fall in love with her – then your heart will open and then you can feel the rhythm of her heart and hear her singing. I am sure there is a note in her song that will be in complete harmony with you, with who you are. That is why you came here in the first place even though you have forgotten!"

Grandfather had finally caught up with the little girl and she awoke from her conversation with Water. The stream just looked a beautiful but ordinary stream again.

"What's up, dear?" asked Grandfather and the little girl told him everything Water had said. He listened carefully to every word and when she had finished, he said, "Wow, that sounds like an amazing experience! Water has just given you a mighty task – to help share her story! I can help you to write it down and then everyone who reads it will be able to help Water too!"

Angelique Rodriguez, Denver Colorado, USA

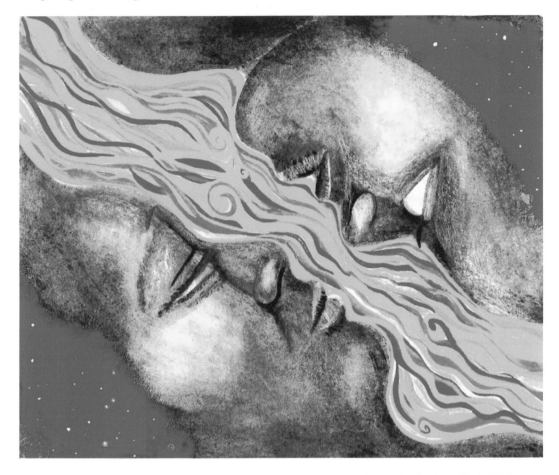

illustration by Anna-Carin Martensson

My name is Angelique Rodrigues and I will be sharing a story I hold deep in my heart which makes it a love story, however it's not like any other love story you've ever heard.

It is my prayer you feel inspired, connected and open to letting your heart waters song, call you home.

We begin our story joining a conversation between The Divine Feminine and her Daughter who is preparing for her journey to Earth in the last days of The Separation.

Please note my reference to 'Men' within this story is a generalized term and does not in this case refer exclusively to the male gender.

This story is dedicated to all the Water Protectors.

REMEMBRANCE

Source Mother: "My love, are you ready for your journey?"

Daughter of the Land: "Yes, I am, but I do have a question, there's something I don't understand. Why do they cause so much suffering, and act as if life doesn't matter?"

Her Mother answers, "Hear me my love. When you become a Daughter of the Earth, You MUST be strong, and have Endurance, for in this cycle they will not understand you. You see, there has been a distortion, a manipulation, about who you are and the gifts you bring. In this distortion, you and I, will both, not be seen as we truly are.

No.

The Divine Feminine energy you hold in pureness and innocence, they will seek to taint and defile.

They will work very hard to convince you that your sensual fluid essence is wrong and shameful.

In this time the eyes of men darken with possession. There is an imbalance that has created a separation casting a shadow over their hearts. These deceitful lies that have been told are designed to keep you separate.

So daughter, stay vigilant or even you may succumb to this blindness and begin to believe the lies that feed the sickness.

The hypnotic dogma that will keep the whole of humanity imprisoned until there is a remembrance."

"In this time,

they will not see your divine beauty,

they will not see your truth,

they will not want to hear your voice of reason.

No, they will be blind and deaf, fearful of your wisdom because they are unable to see.

They have separated me from their hearts, and do not understand that I am a part of them. They have forgotten who they truly are.

They have fallen asleep in their consciousness, and put man's laws higher than Natural Law.

This manipulation of illusion has taken over them. They have defiled the lands, and the waters of their own bodies, polluting their hearts and minds with greed and power.

They do not care that the electric currents are killing Her living waters.

They are aware that by cutting the trees they create desert wastelands, devoid of water and life.

And yet, they will do it for power.

They have been blinded. They have lost their senses, their hearts are closed off and darkened by their lust to dominate.

They stop my flow with their dams and industry altering the land, disturbing the natural rhythms for profit, for paper they will do their job."

They will be convinced that taking by force will bring what their heart desires.

I can tell you for sure, these ways have left them empty inside for their riches cannot feed their soul as I can.

Deep within they can feel something is wrong. They are fearful but they are unsure of what, they are empty and they don't understand why."

"But I will tell you why", her mother goes on, "it is because they killed off the lands that held them so tenderly when they played as children, and polluted the rivers and lakes that held joy, and refreshment for them in their youth. They are lost and have forgotten their way. And now in this age, they look around at the desolation created and they feel scared.

But not scared enough!

For their fear, is not because there are no trees to be held within or clean water to feel refreshed with. No, they fear that there is no more to take, to sell, they fear the loss of profits, threatening the security they found in this illusion.

So, in desperation, they dig, penetrating the Sacred Divine, taking what was not freely offered. Violating natural law, they dig deeper and take more."

The Daughter of the land asks her Mother: "Mother what can I do? Please tell me before I go, tell me what I can do to lift this veil from their eyes, to cast out the shadow that darkens their hearts? Tell me, please Mother, I will do it!"

Source Mother says: "My Sweet child, do your best to remember what I have told you today and stay present! The lies and illusion will be thick to all your senses. It may be hard to remember, but if you listen not with your ears, but with your heart, then I can guide you.

This heart channel, will be the only line of communication we have, once you arrive in the Earth realm.

It's extremely important that you Remember to go to the waters! I will wait for you there. She is your ally. I have sent Her to hold a divine space for all who choose to journey back to me.

She carries my essence in her structure, in Her movement and memory She holds all you'll need for this difficult time, when the birthing pains of labouring a new world will feel absolutely, unbearable. Although it may feel unbearable at times, know that She is my steward.

The waters within have been given, to hold the instructions and guide you in your most difficult times."

"Remember the word 'surrender'. It's the key in your journey of letting go, this may sound like the opposite of what you would do in such a treacherous time.

But know this, you do not stand alone in these times of destruction. I have given you helpers and aid. All you have to do is ask your water.

In these times She will hold you in the Sacred space of Her tenderness and compassion. Just as you feel my love for you now, you will feel my love from Her and through Her. Remember this can only happen from your heart!

So, sit with Her as often as you can, She will help you to remember. Show your respect and give thanks to Her often. Leave the rivers, lakes and shores gifts and prayers. This acknowledgment and demonstration shows Her that you got your instructions from me and that I have sent you, and She will know you are a relative."

Source Mother goes on: "It is critical you feed and take care of your heart. Listen very carefully to what She tells you, for it is my voice you will hear. This is the only way for us to stay connected as you walk through that realm. Be diligent, it will take practice to hear my voice.

For there will be a loudness that permeates into the deepest places of you. You will have to defend your peace with all your might, because they will try to take it from you any chance they get. If you do not, you too will be lost in this illusion of separation like the others. This peace is absolutely necessary to hear my voice in your heart."

Daughter of the Land asks: "How will I know I am hearing you and not the illusion?"

Source Mother says: "You will know I'm there when you feel a connection to your heart water. You will feel safe, serene and peaceful in the deepest places of your being. When you hear the song of your soul it will help you remember.

Do your best to remember what I have told you today. Once there you will have to listen very carefully in your quiet spaces, so protect them well."

The deeper you drop into that space of your heart, the clearer your instructions will be. Follow your hearts song until it echoes in every fibre of your being, then you will know it has led you back to me."

Source Mother goes on: "Daughter, know this history will be rewritten in the hearts and minds of those able to hear my song. This will be the time the men and women of the earth will begin to remember the words.

So, the longer you stay with the waters the easier it will be to hear. Soon the waters within will began to harmonize with the song in your heart. For She is me, and I am Her.

Stay close to the Sacred waters within you and protect them as you do your own heart. Because there is where I have given everyone the blueprints and technology you will need to stop the machines and destruction of this time. The information has been Embedded in your heart, and waters. They must be activated together to open the Sacred scroll within.

So do not look to your leaders, politicians, friends, or lovers for this life saving information."

Daughter of the Land asks: "Mother, will I be able to bring ones I love to this place?"

Source Mother sits quietly, because she knows the deep love that runs through her daughter and answers:

"The design can only work through each one's own individual heart. So, no, my love, you cannot do it for your partner, mother or father, all must make their own journey through their hearts. Following their own song back to the rivers of me.

And You need not worry for the babies or children, for they remain in their hearts and they still listen and follow their waters. They will be there waiting for you.

In this place of the heart, you will find very important instructions in the water. In this sacred space there will be a light. This light will shine so bright it will bring new vision to see the words I have put into the waters. Here is where I have put the instructions of how to move forward at this time."
60

"This is the most important time to protect your hearts PEACE. Because without it you will not be able to activate the light that will allow you to see the living waters instructions.

Listen! Listen very close where heart & water meet in consciousness. Here in this celestial space, you will remember who you truly are. You will remember the structure of love that is embedded in every single molecule of you. Here only truth can reside.

And I promise you there will be no remembrance of the pain and sorrow you have gone through at the hands of those who have not known me. All that you suffered will be given back to you, in blissful joy 100fold. When this cycle is complete, and your birthright restored, then there will be balance on earth. She will heal with you into Her original design in all Her gorgeous beauty and splendor.

You're Lineage from that point, will forever carry these earths codes that brought the great cycle back into harmony. Never again will the living waters of your physical body be forgotten.

This time will be known as the cycle of REMEMBRANCE!

In this new age of remembrance, those who feed on destruction will not live.

For the heart song from our Divine Mother, Water, will be so loud it will pierce their ears and hearts like daggers.

Each will have to choose to learn this new song or go away.

There will be no room or tolerance of anyone who tries to take in an unrighteous way from our Source Mother.

No!

This will be a time of accountability.

At this time, those who hear their heart song will Stand, Unified, Poised and ready to protect their Mother with a righteous indignation and fierceness never seen in time before. Those destroying the earth, will be brought to ruin."

"The Divine Feminine will take her rightful place, completing the cycle of separation and the Earth will rejoice that you are now Her steward.

All will work together in community led wisdom, based in heartfelt Love for their Mother, Earth. This will cause her to flourish in delight, her bounty of gifts and abundance will be given in love and gratitude.

She, will recognize the love for the Divine Feminine that is brought through your hearts nourishing waters and the Age of REMEMBRANCE will be greatly blessed."

In Love and Service I lay this gift with gratitude

my name is Angelique Rodriguez

– Thank you for the contribution you are!

Magnus Pamp, Sweden

illustration by Kia Enbarr

The Water Dream

The Water Inside You, the Life Around You

I feel obligated to share this with you, but also very honoured. It is about an ancient wisdom, today used by people close to Mother Earth but forgotten by so many.

The knowledge is simple and yet so precious. Something that you can easily use in your everyday life.

First, I want to tell you how the knowledge came to me. I have been studying dreamwork for a long time. Ten years ago, I spent one of many weekends with my dream teacher and her other students. As you might know, we use our own dreams during the lessons when we are talking about dreams, learning to use and understand them, and how to practice dream healing.

I arrived the night before the dream course began. During the past week, I had not dreamed of anything I remembered when I woke up. I still wanted my own dream to work with during the weekend so before I fell asleep, I asked for a useful dream during the night. Maybe I just wanted to be a good student, but anyway, I woke up early next morning with a crystal clear, very vivid dream. The feeling in the dream was completely different from what I was used to. It was as if I was there, the real me, and I knew that in this dream I had been given a gift to share with others.

This is the dream that came to me that night:

I am high up on a mountain in the Himalayas. All around me I see countless snow-capped mountain peaks. The moon is shining and the landscape shimmers in a silvery light. In front of me is a large, elongated table made of the purest silver. The tabletop slopes slightly from the left to the right and clean, clear water flows peacefully over the table surface.

On the other side of the table a young monk appears. He is wearing a maroon-coloured robe with an ochre-yellow piece of cloth wrapped around him. The monk makes an invitingly, sweeping gesture with his hand making me understand that I am invited to drink the water. I sit down at the table, bow my head, put my lips to the surface of the water and gently sip some of the cold, fresh water. The water is very shallow, and I do not get much in my mouth. The monk gesticulates for me to move closer to the source of the water.

I get up, walk around the person sitting next to me, and sits down again. This time the monk hands me a drinking glass.

64

Behind the monk, a shimmering image of the Dalai Lama emerges. He smiles mildly. Then the young monk begins to speak, "Here my friend, fill the glass and drink, but before you drink, send your prayers to the water. Pray for what your heart desires, for what you know is wise and pure, pray for what benefits you and the rest of the world. Send your highest wishes to the water. Pray for the healing you need. Pray for the wisdom you desire. Also send your love to the water. Fill the water with as much gratitude as possible. Then drink the water. The water you drink will unify with the water in your body. Your prayers will be spread within you, from cell to cell. You will vibrate with your highest desires. Water is a messenger, a healer, and a transformer. You, my friend, will become a living prayer. The prayer that you, the earth and we all need."

When I woke up the dream was still very vibrant. I hurried to write it down. When we all gathered in the morning, my dream teacher asked if anyone wanted to share a dream from the night before.

I was the only one who had a dream to share. So, I told her about the monk, the water, and the prayers. When I had finished retelling my dream, the dream teacher said:

"Magnus, what you have dreamed is true. What you describe is exactly what I have planned for tonight."

Before we finished for the day, my teacher placed a small, white table in the middle of the circle with participants. A beautiful glass carafe with water was placed on the table, it was surrounded by as many glasses as the number of participants sitting in the circle. Then she said, "Send your highest wishes to the water, drink the water, and let your desires vibrate within you with the help of the water." In my prayer, I asked to communicate the powers of dreams to others and then I drank the water. Through this story, the knowledge and the wisdom of the water is now yours. Use it if you want to and feel free to spread it.

Lina Petersdotter Johansson, Sweden

photo by Lina Petersdotter Johansson

The way of the water

"The way of the water is to always find a way. If you can't trust anything else, you can always trust that; You will always find your way."

As I stood there in Muddus National Park in Norrland, Sápmi, watching the sun rise over the tree tops mirroring itself in the water of the mire beneath my feet those words came whispering through me.

The mire always astonishes me. The way it erases the boundaries. It symbolises the union of flesh and spirit. Where does the earth start and where does the water end?

Maybe that's why the mire has always made me feel the most at home in the world. Because it's both earth and water.

Something in me becomes whole and when I long for home, that's where my heart goes.

So I trusted that water will always find the way and allowed it to guide me on my journey home. Home to my roots and to retrieve my inner wild child which I had lost.

I hadn't been home to the north of Sweden properly in many years but now I knew it was time. Time to come home and to bring myself home.

I took two weeks off and started driving. Knowing only where to stop the first night and knowing that I needed to go all the way to the mires of Sjaunja, where I'd left that part of me, the wild child, longing to come home. Letting the water and my heart lead the way.

I stopped everyday by a lake or stream to bathe, no matter how cold it was. Cleansing myself deeply from the stories which I'd carried with me. From my childhood, from my teenage years and from my adult life. All the stories about not being enough or being too much. All the stories about who I had to be and who I'm not allowed to be. All the stories which were not serving me anymore. I bathed and asked the water to help me to release all that wasn't mine. To set me free.

After the bath I always asked to know where to go next. Which water to connect with, where to stop for the night. The water gave me the directions I needed and I kept going. For days I travelled through the long country which is called Sweden, the country which I call my home.

I drove, I bathed, I released, I cried and I drove some more. Until the dark fell upon me. Then I found somewhere to rest. By the water which was willing to hold me during the night.

Trusting the water to guide me home. Home to my roots, to myself, to the wild child which I'd left by the mires and lake of Sjaunja so many years ago.

Finally arriving at the place of my start in this life, the village of Allavaara at the start of Sjaunja nature reserve, this strange feeling of not knowing the grounds yet also knowing exactly where to go hit me. I was safe. I was home. Yet had only spent the first three years of my life there. Still those years gave me my roots. Created the fundament which later developed in to me.

"You are lucky to have roots", the Sápmi artist Elin Teilus told me in a conversation we had about longing for home, "Most people don't", and maybe that's why we are drifting so far away from ourselves, because we are so unrooted. Cause even if I've lived far away from my roots for a long time, I've always been able to feel and connect with them. Always known that they are there. In a sense I think that has always given me a feeling of safety. A knowing that I'm always home, no matter where in the world because water connects us all.

Now, setting my feet on the soil where my roots are deepest connected I could also connect with the water of this place. I became whole, once more.

Bjorn, who was a young man when we moved from Allavaara greeted me with a smile. He could remember me and my family and showed me around with fondness. I got to see the cabin I spent my first years in and enjoy the beautiful scenery. But mostly I longed to go down to the lake.

When I was finally there I put up my tent and stepped down to the lake for my ceremonial bath as I had done so many times before. Not knowing in my mind what needed to be done for this ceremony but trusting my body and guides. On the way down I found two feathers. One from a crow and one from an eagle. I asked them to help me. To cleanse myself from all that I needed to let go of, and to connect with the courage and wisdom to meet and do my inner wild child right. I laid them on a stone in the water, called up on that lost wild child of mine and asked her to re-join my body once more. Then I laid down in the cold water. Resigning to life yet again.

After a short while I could feel a tingling sensation in my body and hear her voice inside my heart. It was a joyous feeling of reconnecting but I could also hear the sharpness in her voice:

"Only if you make room for me. I'm a part of you which can't compromise. For me to survive I can't be anything than myself, fully."

I took a deep breath and swallowed hard, knowing that this would lead to a big, important and sometimes challenging shift. She continued:

"And I'm not satisfied with just being heard as many of the other parts of you. Just seeing me is not enough, I need physical action too."

68

"I need you to embrace me with your whole and allow me to speak, to act and to live. Without cages or shackles. Otherwise I'd rather want you to leave me here. Where I can roam wild and free."

"I hear you and I honour you and so it shall be" I said and took yet another deep breath. Embraced the cold once more, opened up my heart and dived down to the bottom of the lake with the intention of breaking the surface together with my wild child.

As I slowly walked out of the water. I knew, life had just begun.

Marie Bech, Sweden

illustration by Marie Bech

How Water came to Earth

It was a silent night, no wind shaking the leaves or bending the grass. It was one of those nights were no clouds floated in the sky, leaving everything in the sky visible.

It was one of those nights when it felt like you could see all the stars in the entire and vast Universe and even though they are eons away, they seemed so close, almost as if you could reach out and touch them and if you listened closely, you could hear them sing to each other.

We were all sitting in a Circle around the fire, stories were shared, like they had been for generations, since the dawn of time. When all the stories were shared, right before it was time to go home, a question was asked by the voice of a young girl:

"– Where did water come from?"

After a moment in complete silence, Grandmother Willowroot replied:

"–Water came to Earth with the Stars."

"–Did they really, but how, the Stars live in the sky, so how could they possible have brought water to us?" the young girl asked further.

"–Well now little girl, the hour is late and we should all go to bed" answered Grandmother.

"–But please, please, I have so many dreams about Water, I am so curious and I won't be able to sleep now" the girl said.

Grandmother Willowroot got up and put on new logs of wood in the almost burnt out fire. She reached into her leather pouch, carried around her neck at all times. She took out a Starfish carved of bone, it was so white it was glowing like a star in the light from the fire.

She looked at it, touched it with her fingertips.

"I was gifted this as a young girl when I was told the story about water. It was gifted as a reminder of how precious the gift of Water is, and to always remember and honour that."

71

She closed her hand around the Starfish. "Listen closely and I will share the story of how Water came to Earth.

A long time ago, when the Creator was putting the Earth together, before it was even possible to walk the Earth, the element of Fire ruled. Fire was so powerful, everything was burning, glowing and hissing. Volcanoes, constantly erupting, covering the ground with vast lava lakes and rivers of molten lava. It's beauty was breathtaking, but however beautiful it was, the Creator realized that it would not be possible to put plants, animals, birds, fishes, insects or humans on the Earth as it was now.

Realizing help was needed, the Creator asked the Universe if someone would volunteer to do the honourable task of bringing Water to Earth?

The Stars were the first to volunteer, to take on this rather huge challenge:

'– We would be honoured to do it' they said unanimous.

All though the Creator was very grateful to the Stars" Grandmother continued, "concern came into his mind. Stars are immense spheres of heat and gas, in a fiery dance, and as soon as they would even come near water or Ice, it would evaporate into thin air.

Even so, the Creator thanked the Stars and told them to wait until enough Water was gathered to balance the element of Fire on Earth.

Years and years passed, the Creator had been very busy collecting Water, converting it into Ice for it to be more easy to bring to the Earth. Much thought had been given as how the Stars would be able to carry the Ice, without melting it.

The Stars requested a meeting with the Creator, since they had not heard anything in a rather long time.

'– Did you know that we have relatives, living on other planets?' the Stars said.

The Creator looked surprised by their question and said: 'No, I had no idea.'

'We want to introduce to you, the Starfish, one of our closest relatives, living in a distant corner of the Universe. It took them a long time to come here' did the Stars inform."

Grandmother continued "– One of the Starfish approached the Creator, it's beauty was striking as it introduced itself:

'– A long time ago, we were the ones who brought Water to the antient planet we come from. At that time, we were transformed from Stars into Starfish by our Creator. I brought some of the elixir we were given and now, I offer it to You' the Starfish said.

The Creator reached out and accepted the gracious gift from the Starfish. As soon as the bottle touched his hands, all the Starfish disappeared.

The Creator paused for a moment before he asked:

'– Are you all ready to become Starfish and bring Water to Earth?'

'–Yes, we are ready!' said the Stars and one by one they came forward to get a drop of the elixir. As soon as the droplet touched the surface of the Star, it turned into a Starfish. The last Star was given the bottle with the remaining elixir to maybe one day give as a gift to other Stars.

All the new born Starfish was given a pearl of Ice. The Creator put the pearl in the centre of each Starfish where they could hold on to it with their arms. He then gave them instructions on how and where to deposit the Ice pearls once they reached Earth. They went on their long journey through space to Earth.

They circled the planet to wait for all to arrive, then, one by one, the Starfish dropped their pearl of ice on top of the mountains of lava. As the pearls melted there were little streams of Water, running down to the open landscape, where they created lakes and rivers.

As the Earth cooled, vast oceans spread around the globe. The element of Fire sank into the core of the Earth where the icy Water could not reach it.

Starfish fell in love with the Oceans and made them their new home. Happy and content they sang the starfish song to Water and to Fire who now could exist on Earth in balance."

"This is how Water came to the Earth, so remember when you see a Starfish, they are the ones who brought Water, when you see a star in the sky, they were part of it too."

Grandmother Willowroot looked around the Circle, she looked deep into the eyes of the little girl:

"– Come here little one." The girl came up to her, her bright eyes were shining together with the Stars in the sky.

"– I want to give you this!" Grandmother handed over the Starfish to the girl.

"– Now you are the carrier of the Sacred Starfish and the legend of Water. You will carry it and share it's story forward to the next generations to come".

Dorianne Daniels, Mukulu

illustration by Dorianne Daniels

Mosi-oa-Tunya

There is a magical place called, Mosi-oa-Tunya. The Smoke That Thunders. It crosses over two nations, Zambia and Zimbabwe. It is the largest waterfall on the planet. I visited, Mosi-oa-Tunya (The Victorian Falls) years ago, in my dream time. I walked on her green pastures. There were others drawn to this sacred land, from many different cultures. I looked ahead and I was in awe of what I saw. A chasm in the Earth that stretched wide and deep. Cascading over the chasm was the biggest waterfall I have ever seen in my life. I have seen quite a few in the land in which I now live, Australia and also in New Zealand but nothing compared to this incredible waterfall.

I was in disbelief as I watched on in the dark night. The full Moon shone in all her glory. Perfectly arched over the waterfall was a brilliant rainbow. The ancients called me to this land to remember my roots. To remember the songs of my ancestral home, the many truths and mysteries that lay in this ancient African landscape that lives on in my bones. My time at Mosi-oa-Tunya was short but her impact on my being has been etched in my heart forever.

As I sit with Mosi-oa-Tunya in contemplation, I sense the Heart of the Earth pulsating, rhythmic and alive. The rushing water hits the rocks below so powerfully that the sound is like thunder. It is said that you can hear the thunder of the water up to 40km away. As I meditate and visualise this incredible waterfall I imagine the Earth taking a long, deep inhaling breath, she is in pure ecstasy from the soothing and joyful sensation that water gives her. As the Earth exhales smoke, from the mist of the water arises from the deep cavern below and billows up like incense.

The waters of Mosi-oa-Tunya teach us that though our hearts may be pounded again and again by heartbreak and loss, our hearts can never truly be broken or destroyed. It is from the heart break that the heart opens up and experiences a greater sense of joy, love, peace and ecstasy. When we let go and stop resisting, when we unclench the fist

and accept reality as it is now, transformation occurs. Mosi-oa-Tunya clearly demonstrates this truth as her powerful rushing waters transform into the smoke that rises.

Water all over the Earth and within our very own body says – feel the currents, feel the waves, feel the stillness, feel the ebb and feel the flow. Feel everything that you are. When you are swept up in the turbulence of life, let go as surfers do when they are swallowed up by the white water. They tuck themselves into a foetal position and surrender into the womb of the ocean. As they tumble over and over, still they surrender in complete trust. You too can learn to do the same in daily life. When times are stressful, challenging, or your heart is broken or your soul troubled, you can let go and let yourself feel the torrents of life as you hold fast to the abiding peace and trust in your heart and the Yogis of India remind us of, Anahata, the unstruck heart that lives within all sentient beings.

The following story is a fairytale, my own personal creation story. Water is not only asking us to feel but to express. Water asks us to feel all that we are so that we do not crush the creative impulse that is always available to us. Is it time that you let go of your serious mind so that you can come into your own creative soulful expression? We often ask children to do this but playtime for adults is just as important for our wellbeing. Would you take a moment to write about water that speaks to you and possibly draw a picture about it?

I am no artist yet I feel incredibly proud of my drawing of Mosi-oa-Tunya and my connection to this ancient land of my ancestors. The drawing speaks to me on many levels.

Go on and surprise yourself, write, draw, dance, sing or sound and connect with your creative essence.

The Story of Water and Earth by Mukulu

In the darkness where nothing existed was Awareness. Awareness overlooked all the worlds and indeed was part of everything in existence. One day a rock hurtled through space.

The rock caught alight as it neared the Sun's rays. The Sun smiled as he watched the young rock burn brightly with his àṣẹ*, passion and will.

The rock had never felt this sensation before, she was burning hot and longed to be cooled. Awareness observed the distress of the burning rock and felt deep compassion. Love arose in its heart for this young one that was so pure and innocent.

A single drop of water dropped from Awareness eye. The tear rolled down Awareness cheek and finally dropped from her chin. The teardrop landed heavily on rock. It fell so hard it caused a giant crack to form and opened rock's heart. As more and more tears fell, a long wide ridge formed.

Rock was filled with gratitude for water's embrace.

The water gathered in size and speed as it moved and became a giant waterfall that cascaded down the ridge.

Water hit the heart of rock so powerfully that the sound was like thunder. Rock took a long, deep inhaling breath. She was in pure ecstasy from the soothing and joyful sensation water gave her.

As rock exhaled smoke rose from the deep cavern that billowed up like incense.

Day turned to night, as stars gathered close and shone in awe of the beauty of rock. Grand Mother Moon was thrilled to hear whispers, "a new life comes".

The ever green trees and plants that formed on rocks surface was perfect. She smiled down on rock. Suddenly a truly magical thing occurred. A rainbow, bigger and brighter than any other that ever shone before or after, stretched out and arched over the waterfall.

From that night on rock was named Earth. Earth birthed many life forms, from the lifegiving water that came from Awareness and she rejoices in each and every one of them.

Today if you were to visit Mosi-oa-Tunya, The Smoke That Thunders, in Zambia or Zimbabwe and if you happened to be there on the night of a full Moon, you would see what rock saw millions of years ago; Grand Mother Moon shining down on her face as the Rainbow arches over her waterfall, crowning her Mother Earth, Mother of all.

* *àṣẹ - is a word that people all over the world who follow the path of African Spirituality use, which explain in the following words – power and will. I felt it important to use as a way of re-membering one of humanity's oldest languages that in South Africa, many slaves who were brought down from West Africa were forced to give up and take on a new language.*

Camilla Hjortdal Sindahl

The Waterfall That Stopped Falling

Once upon a time, there was a mighty waterfall. From it, sprang dozens of little streams, big rivers, and smaller waterfalls, spreading out into a great area of land. This water went to several small villages, lying like pearls on a string on the riverbanks. The people living there had a great life and lived in harmony with each other. They did not think so much about where the water came from – the water had always been there, and the knowledge of the great waterfall supplying them with fresh water every day seemed forgotten. Until one remarkable day when they truly came to understand water's worth.

illustrations by Lone Aabrink

80

But…. before that day, something else needed to happen: The discovery of the mighty waterfall. A man living in a village nearby, was hiking in the mountains, as he almost stumbled upon it. He did not pay so much attention to the waterfall though, but more to what he found in the water below it… gold! Gold and more gold, glowing like stars at the stony bottom of the little pond. He was utterly amazed. He gathered the little community of villages together and told them what treasure he had found. They were all excited. Real gold! What an adventure! Everyone went out to see it for themselves, and even though most only noticed the gold, the villagers had arrived at the waterfall.

There was a little boy, he did not understand all the fuss about the gold. He was much more interested in the waterfall. As everyone had followed the stream to arrive here, he asked, "Does our water come from here?" His mother nodded and smiled. "Yes, and now we have all this gold! This must be a gift to us from the Gods. We are incredibly lucky" she said.

Arriving at the waterfall, they collected the gold, as much as they could carry in their hands and pockets. Still, there was plenty more gold. The boy, playing in the water near the waterfall, suddenly felt unease. It was like the waterfall had become paler. As he was still so young, he did not have words to describe it, so he said nothing. As they returned home, he looked at the water flowing in the great river and felt sad. The little boy said to his mother, "I do not want to forget the waterfall." His mother looked at him; in that moment, she had an idea.

Out of the gold, she had a beautiful water faucet made. She was pleased – the boy seemed happy now and she had found something to do with the gold. In all honesty, their little family did not want for anything. In fact, nobody in the community of small villages needed the gold. So, when the word got out that a beautiful gold water faucet had been made, everybody wanted one.

It became a fad, some even had golden sinks and bathtubs made. Little by little, the villagers picked up the gold from the waterfall to make golden toilets and golden showers – until one day, there was no gold left to mine.

So now, we are getting closer to the day when the people started to pay attention to the real gift given to them. That morning, after the last gold had been collected, the man who found the gold in the first place woke up wanting a shower, a cup of coffee, a sip of water, but… no water came. He went to his neighbour; it was the same there. They went from house to house, slowly realizing that it was the same everywhere. The river had gone dry. How could that have happened? They followed the dry riverbed to see if they could solve the problem. They ended up at the waterfall, and what a surprise they found! The waterfall had simply stopped flowing. Right in the middle of its fall, as though locked in time, the flow of the water had stopped – causing all the rivers to run dry.

It was unbelievable! Someone talked about it being a curse. But why would the Gods first give them gold and then take away their water supply? "It doesn't make any sense," they thought. The little boy had followed along, and now he had a weird feeling in his stomach. It was clear to him now – the waterfall was lacking its colors completely now.

"I think the waterfall is sad", he said. "Maybe it did not want us to take the gold?" The villagers looked at each other: Yes, that could be the case. They seemed to miss the point, because instead of trying to really understand what had happened, they got angry. What madness! Why would the waterfall trick them in this way? They demanded, "Start to flow, we need the water! Come on, stupid waterfall!" But nothing happened. The water remained frozen in midair. The villagers left, feeling sadness and anger. The boy lagged behind. He wept for his parents and the whole community. Water was essential for them.

As his tears fell into the riverbed, he thought about what helped him feel better; his mom gently asking him "What's the matter?" and making it clear that she was there for him if he needed to talk. So, he did what he had learned through her example. He sat down in front of the waterfall and asked, "Why are you sad? I am here to listen if you want my help".

You won't believe it, but the waterfall began to speak: "Little human. Throughout time, the people living close have been traveling here to give thanks and to pray that the water would keep on flowing. Recently, your people have forgotten this."

"Still, I do not need much. I have received so many gifts that I've been passing on to you. In this way, your people have lived on the thankfulness and humbleness of the ones who came before. They gave so much and expected so little.

Your people take the gifts of life for granted, and have forgotten humility, neglected to give thanks and love in return. It is not that I do not want to help you, little human, but I simply cannot. Without appreciation for my efforts, I do not have the energy that is needed to flow."

The waterfall once again became silent. The boy went home, full of sadness. Now not weeping for himself or the community, but for the waterfall that did not have enough life-force to flow.

He went to sleep, but was awakened by nightmares of golden water faucets that drank all the water in the world. He got up, went to the bathroom, and made a decision. He took down his mother's golden water faucet and smashed it into a million pieces.

Walking out into the night, he did not stop until he reached the waterfall. He poured the million shards of gold into the water and said, "Please take this offering of gold back with my gratitude and love, so you can once again shine and be full of life."

The boy went home. The rest of his sleep was peaceful and calm. In the morning, his mom awoke and saw her water faucet missing. She went to the little boy's room, and asked him what happened. The boy was prepared for this, and he explained what had happened truthfully. His mother listened, as only a mother can, and she now understood that the boy had done well. She gathered the community and on behalf of her son, she told his story. People were sceptical, but they were also desperate. They needed the water as they needed the air. One by one, everybody took down their golden showers, toilets, faucets, and tiles. Together, they set out for the waterfall, loaded with gold. They laid the gold back into the waters where it had been taken. They expected the water to immediately start flowing… Nothing happened. They waited and waited, but the waterfall was still frozen. In the end, they lost their patience and went home, now more worried than ever before.

Again, the boy stayed behind. Had he been mistaken, tricked by the water? He sat down, looking out on the water and the gold, trying to remember what the waterfall had said to him. Tired and heavy of heart, he dozed off. In-between awake and asleep, he saw his ancestors at the waterfall kneeling, laying down gold and other treasures in the water.

"Give thanks and prayer," they said. Their words hung in the air as he awakened. He ran home and determinedly found what he thought to be the most precious belonging he had — a crystal given to him by his great, great grandmother. He went back to the waterfall, laid the shiny stone in the water and said, "Please take this gift of thanks and hear my prayer, so that you once again will flow with fresh water." Nothing happened.

As he walked back into the village, he sat out looking at the river. He sat there, vigilant, until night came and he fell asleep on the ground, exhausted.

Now we have arrived to the day when the villagers finally understood: they, for too long, had been mistakenly thinking earth's gifts belonged to them, when in fact earth and man belonged to each other.

In the morning, the boy awoke to the sound of something sorely missed… the sound of flowing water. He stood up. The whole village was there, looking at him, then at the water, then back at him. They inquired about what had happened. The boy told them about what the waterfall had instructed and about his ceremony. The villagers nodded, sat down at the riverbank, and cried tears of joy for the water's return.

For the last time in this tale, the villagers went to the waterfall, carrying gifts of prayer to the waterfall. But it was not the last time in their own story, for they kept on returning, again and again, with gifts of thankfulness and prayer. As for the boy? Well, he was chosen to be the protector of the waterfall. Even though the waterfall never spoke to him again, he could always see its colors to determine if it needed a little more love and care.

This concludes the story about how the balance was restored in this little part of the world. How did I get to know it? Well, let's just say that a mighty, golden, flowing friend told me once.

The end x

Michael V. Coles, Vancouver B.C. Canada

illustration by Anna-Carin Martensson

A Water Well Story

In a small community there was but one aquafer that flowed beneath the land and only one Well that had been dug to catch the river of life for the community.

This Well had been built long before the eldest of them.

One day a new comer bought a piece of land close to the village and started to drill a Well into the land. Some weeks later the community Well was not retaining water. The community soon realized that the water had been redirected due to the second Well being drilled.

They came together to let the new comer know about the problem with the Well water. The new comer explained that it was not his problem since he was not a part of the community.

The community was perplexed with the reasoning of the new comers attitude that they became angrier and angrier every time they heard his repeated reply. It is not my problem.

Soon the shortages became shorter and shorter until the water was no longer and the well dried up. The community soon was force to ask the new comer for water.

The new comer agreed to allow the community to have their fill of water for a price for 0.10c per gallon. The community decided that they would pay the price as long as they could take as much as they wanted.

The new comer was envisioning all the wealth that would be made from this deal that he immediately said Yes, take as much as you want.

With the deal in hand, the community built a pipe from his well to their Well and started pumping. Up the well, across the land and down into the communities well they pumped until the Well was the fullest that it had ever been.

Days and weeks went by, the new comer was so happy collecting his profit from the community.

One day, the water meter stopped turning. The water pipe had become dry. The new comer looked into his Well only to see that it was bone dry.

After days of waiting and still no sign of water, the new comer had to tell everyone the bad news about the water and the lack of.

The new comer went to the community to tell them that they could not continue to use the water until it had replenished itself. When he arrived there, he immediately noticed everyone was still getting water from the Well.

He slowly approached the Well only to see it full to the top. He asked the elder standing near how this was possible. The elder turned and said we used the water to call the river.

The new comer did not understand the elder, then turned to another at the Well for an explanation.

A child came to the front of the line and told the new comer it was a lesson to be learned,

"The flow of life will always take the shortest route to connect with itself.

So when we took the water a long way via pipes and heights until it got tired of the long way home, it took a short cut back to this well.

You must Always Be Well with the Well you have your bucket in or you end up with none".

Anna-Katariina Hollmerus, Finland

The return of the salmon

Harmony was a young woman living close to a beautiful river.

In the old times there used to be salmon wandering up in the stream, happily and gladly jumping out of the water.

The indigenous people used to sing the salmon back every spring with a special song. An old grandmother kept the tradition of singing the salmon song each morning. When she passed, the song for the salmons went with her and no one remembered the song.

From that day on the salmon disappeared from the river and did not come back.

One day the young Harmony was woken up by the spirits of the river. They told her to go early in the morning to the river and sit there. Sit there by a tree close to water in silence. Sit there in silence until she can hear a song. Harmony did so for many days.

On the last day a song appeared in the silence and she started singing it. The song came from between the worlds and was born in silence.

From that day Harmony went every morning at the same time to the river to sing that song for the river.

She did so for over 30 years.

After one year the salmon returned to the river with great joy. And now the salmon is back. Harmony herself got old and is asking: "Who will be the next salmon song singer?"

Are you the next salmon song singer?

Epilogue

by Anna-Carin Martensson

For me this project started in 2010 when I had my first deep encounter with Water. I participated in a course called "Spiritual Ecology", held by Jonathan Horwitz and Zara Waldeback. The meeting with Water changed my whole perception of everything.

We had all been instructed to go out and make contact with water. We should be quiet and focused and we had a couple of hours available for our interaction with water.

Water sprinkled down from the sky as if to meet us. My first thought was to go down to the river and swim to get even more physical contact.

Wearing a bikini and raincoat, I enjoyed splashing barefoot on the wet summer hot asphalt. I focused my thoughts as much as I could on water and started to walk towards the river.

Just before entering the course, I had read some chapters in an anatomy book of nursing education. According to it, 98% of the body's molecules contain water – that is a big part of us indeed! I thought about what would be left if water was removed; desert landscapes and withering plants came to my mind. Without water no life in other words.

When I came down to the river, I remembered that Jonathan had previously asked us not to swim alone. –Yes of course, we have to respect water! I did not think of that at first. As far as I know, no one has died from too much air, but with water it is another story!

The swim had to wait until later but I stood in the water completely captivated by all the swirls the water made at every rock or turn in the river. The water is one body and pulls itself along, but can still be divided into drops of all possible sizes. Then suddenly, when I was standing there, something unusual happened to my consciousness. I felt the water looking at me as much as I was looking at her.

The water felt crystal clear and distinct like a very intelligent being. So intelligent that I blushed. I felt stupid and embarrassed that I had not before understood that water is alive. In a moment that could not have been longer than a second, I realized that water knows exactly what she is doing when she curls like a snake down mountains and hills. She washes and purifies the air when she falls like rain as she gives life to earth on her way to the sea. It is no coincidence that seawater is salty, because water uses salt to purify herself. The sun and water cooperate and distill her on her way up to the sky, where she forms clouds before the next circle. On her way down to the sea, she swirls happily past rocks and stones, she knows how to create energy and is happy to share it with us! Water is alive and she always wants to be in motion. She does not like to be locked in.

She always does her job whether outside or inside ourselves. If we are tired and worn out, we can cleanse and fill ourselves with new energy with water. Letting tears fall when we are burdened by fears or sorrows is a relief and makes us lighter in heart and mind.

Water does all this for us. Always. But we barely see it. Water wants respect. She wants recognition and at least a thank you now and then.

Floods and droughts are not something that water does to harm us. It is simply a consequence of us not seeing or trying to understand the essence of water. We do not respect her need for movement or that her winding roads down the mountains are roads chosen with care. We move rivers and build dams as it suits us. We rinse oil tankers and flush medicines down the toilet. We are cooling the nuclear power plants with her. We turn on the shower faucet as if it were our right and nothing to be grateful for.

Not until we humble ourselves enough to slow down and listen to what water has to teach can we learn to live in balance and harmony.

A good start is to say – Thank you!

All this came to me in an instant and changed my view of everything for the rest of my life!

In 2020 the feeling grew that I wanted to do something more to give back to Water. It came to me that we are living in a culture where the natural connection to nature is very weak, almost lost, and that is why it is so easy for us humans to see her just as a resource to use as we like, instead of listening to her with the intent of finding out how we can cooperate.

We need to find the connection I think we once had. We need a collective change of our way of thinking if we are going to find a sustainable way of living.

When contemplating on this I thought that perhaps if people who are in a deep relationship with water tell a story from their heart perhaps it can touch the heart of others, so I called out for people to tell their stories of water.

In just a few days we became a group of 25 people, most of us were totally strangers of each other. 16 of us have now shared our stories and a couple shared their pictures. This has been a joyful work of trust between us all, and I am so happy that all responded to my, or more accurate Water's call. What we have experienced when listening to Water is very similar and after reading all stories the message stands clear:

Water is life!

Love her, respect her, protect her and sing and laugh with her.

She needs our love!

THE WATER PROJECTS WE SUPPORT

All proceeds from the sale of this book are split in equal shares. All writers got one share and one share was decided to go to a project that will benefit the work for Water in some way. Several of the writers decided to donate their shares, so we support two organisations instead of one. Those organisations are very different but they both are aiming towards a sustainable way of living in right relations with All Living beings.

World Water Community

~Doing the Great Work to Heal Our Waters~

The World Water Community is an online community platform dedicated to supporting the global-to-local healing and restoration of our planetary, and internal, Waters. The Community welcomes all individuals, communities, organizations, businesses and institutions who are passionate about collaborating and sharing knowledge, experience and resources for a world with healthy and thriving Water.

World Water Community provides a diverse ecosystem of tools and spaces for all members to bring this vision into action and reality. We aim to facilitate interaction, collaboration, and sharing of knowledge and resources by bringing all water related activities to one place, with social groups, messaging, blogs, directories of water organizations, a water related events calendar, a learning management system for water related courses, a multivendor marketplace (for sharing, selling, and loaning), a crowdfunding platform for projects by community members, and other resources to come.

The vision for the World Water Community platform started to grow when my partner and I were attending the yearly water conferences for my water vitalization research. Participants from diverse backgrounds created the most beautiful and friendly atmosphere. They were not only scientists, but also inventors, entrepreneurs, healthcare providers, artists, and more.

What they had in common was a fascination for water and an open mind for unusual ideas, solutions, and theories. For all attendees it was always very inspiring and helpful to meet likeminded souls, and to know who is working on what, to find collaborators and combine efforts.

Since most of what is shared there is new or out of the box, it is vital to be able to communicate and further spread what these solutions can bring on all levels, such as water quality, health, vitality, plants, ecosystems, energy, awareness, consciousness, as well as relational, societal, and so much more… So this is where our drive to create bridges between practical applications and scientific understanding and 'the world' was born… And when the funds for the Water Research Lab I worked at ran out (a scenario not uncommon for this type of water science… and one of the reasons we need to share resources and collaborate), I was free to start making our vision a reality, so my partner and I invested savings and time in building the platform.

We believe that what we have collectively seen with water science, and also in all of our combined life's experiences as beautifully displayed in this book, has the potential to heal the world! If one truly understands that water 'has memory', is a transmitter and receiver, 'listens' and reacts to the environment, has unlimited forms and functions, and that water connects all, we will behave differently in relation to our bodily waters, as well as to our fellow water bodies, and the actual physical bodies of water on our planet…

Our aim is to facilitate the realization of collaborative scientific, experimental, theoretical, and practical developments around water in all its facets, to host community led quality guidance for solutions, raised water awareness, teaching, and sharing, for projects in all areas, from art to ecosystem restoration, from consciousness to health, from natural to technical solutions, in order to do the Great Work to Heal Our Waters.

This Great Work is an inner journey as much as an outer journey, an individual as well as a collective exploration, in our opinion best shared in a community with likeminded souls.

We welcome all ideas, input, and support to improve our dynamic platform. We believe in the limitless human potential, and the more diverse we are, the more borders we cross, the more disciplines we bridge, the more impact we have. Water shows us the way…

Our values are related to water's properties… water is the source, it's transparent, inclusive, open, independent and uniting, connecting, dynamic, transmitting and receiving, and always has impact, slow or fast moving, even one drop at a time...

It feels like water is asking us to collaborate now, without boundaries, cross-discipline, to heal ourselves and the world. It's a calling for all voices to be heard! Through the resources on the platform anyone with passion for water has the opportunity to spread and develop their impactful contribution.

Thank you so much for creating 'Stories of Water', it sets a wonderful example for a collaborative project that ignites the fire for water (water burns too! ☺). We will support in any way we can to keep your movement going!

–With much gratitude and respect for all the water in and around us,,Everine van de Kraats

Co-founder World Water Community, Water Scientist

Please visit the website to find out what kind of functionalities are available in World Water Community:

https://www.worldwatercommunity.com

Nurture The Children, NTC, History and Vision

I started *Nurture The Children* (NTC) in 1992; although at that time it was just *Grandma Carole's Games and Storytime*. I started because as I attended Pow-Wow's I noticed that there was little being done to educate the children about Native American Culture.

I started by providing games based on the basic skills native children would need to survive. I invited the children (native and non-native) to join me in my time machine and travel back 500 years to the time before the coming of European influence. The games I start with are designed to teach about the strong connection between Native People and the Earth Mother. I believe in teaching our children by "nurturing through nature".

We play the:
1. Moving Camp Game where the children are required to use their most important Indian tool…their imagination. If you can imagine it, you can make it happen. They traveled from winter camp down in the valley to summer camp up in the mountain.
2. The Rattle Snake game teaches listening skills.
3. Fire Tender teaches the sacred nature of fire, sneak-up & listening skills.

¬ 1997 ~ School Programs began. I believe all knowledge belongs to the children and therefore I cannot "sell" it. The school programs provided another opportunity.

¬ 2000 ~ Youth Serving Youth Programs began with the first Annual Rosebud Relief Clothing Drive. We now have annual clothing drives ~ annual school supply drives ~annual the coat and boot drive and any special project NTC is working on. All proceeds go to Rosebud, Reservation, S.D. Each year we focus on a different community.

¬ We have done a couple of special projects; new textbooks for Spring Creek Elementary School and over 3,000 books to start a "library" at He Dog School; sadly, He Dog School still only has a reading room because there are no funds for a librarian.

¬ 2011 First annual Water is Life Walk ~ now planning the 11th annual.

Why Water Walks? Nothing lives without Water and the majority of reservations have a lack of clean water, mostly due to Environmental Racism. To nurture our children, we first most take care of Mother Earths Life Blood the Sacred Water.

It takes so much more than food clothing and shelter to nurture our children. I have found that Nature has been my biggest source of understanding. My first "best friend" was a huge old oak tree that I would climb and share all my secrets with. I have found so much comfort, and fulfillment by sitting upon the Earth Mother and feeling her energy flow up through me and out. Learning to speak without words to the standing one, four-legged, winged ones, creepy crawlers, fined ones and swimmers was the most fulfilling event in my life. I learned how insignificant I am in the Great Mystery. While discovering how insignificant I am I was able to see that there is a place just for me within the "web of life" and that no one can fill that place of responsibility but me. I believe that by helping our children reconnect with the Earth Mother they too can make these discoveries about themselves. Finding their humility and responsibility will help them develop a strong cultural connection, the very basis for a strong personal identity.

With the rising suicide rates among our young people my desire to nurture through nature has become stronger each year. I feel like the small impact made by Youth Serving Youth Programs is like spitting on a prairie fire, making a small local impact that is quickly overcome by the advancing flames.

Strong children form strong families, strong families form strong communities, strong communities form strong Nations and strong nations form a strong worldwide force that can change the very world we live in….one child at a time!

Youth Serving Youth programs started when I saw the opportunity to connect Youth on and off the reservation. Providing a way for those more fortunate to serve the children on the reservation this also provides an opportunity for cultural exchange.

I have never been disappointed by the willingness of our youth to become involved. Once they are offered the opportunity they step forward and respond beyond my expectations. I see these programs as having a threefold objective.

1. Educating mainstream America about the fact that Native American children living on and off reservations do not have the same educational possibilities as even the poorest person living within mainstream American society.

2. Educating mainstream America about the poverty in Indian Country

3. By teaching young children to serve others provides the opportunity to feel the fulfillment of spirit (that intangible element that one gets from service to others). They will then continue to serve others throughout their lives. The children's nation (native and non-native) needs to be nurtured through nature if we are to have any hope of healing the Earth Mother.

–What is it that NTC does now that you believe most embodies what you were trying to accomplish when you had the initial vision for NTC?

The school programs help to bring about an understanding and acceptance of the diversity and value of traditional earth ways. The Youth Serving Youth programs provide an opportunity to put diversity education to the test. When the youth reach out to serve others that they will never see they develop the ability to "see" past their differences.

This dominant culture starts teaching their children in preschool with little tests that ask them to "circle the thing that is different, circle the one that doesn't belong".
Weather it is an intentional lesson or not by the time they are in third grade they understand that "If they are different, they do not belong." We must provide opportunities for the children to "see" that no two things in nature are exactly alike, no two stone, no two shells, not two trees, no two bears…so why should two humans be exactly alike. By helping them discover the beauty in the differences they will begin to accept each other.

Each of them is one leaf on the tree of life, each independently feeding the tree and being fed by the tree but they are also feeding each other because the tree takes what it is given and shares it with all. Each fall thousands of human beings travel great distances to enjoy the beauty of the changing colors found in leaves, yet these same human beings walk past all the beauty of the diversity that surrounds them everyday.

Nature has such powerful lessons to teach us all, but we first must get out there and open our eyes and ears. Learning to see with our ears and hear with our eyes; when I see my cat outside and he opens his mouth I hear with my eyes that he is speaking to me and when I hear the wolf crying in the night I see him with my ears as clearly as if he were right in front of me. We do it everyday without thinking but when we do it with the knowledge that we are doing it, a whole new reality appears.

–What challenges or opportunities, as I like to call them, are facing you now?

Until now I have been a one-woman task force, gathering the children and providing the education and opportunities to serve.

Right now, I am actively seeking members for a board of directors, to make bigger changes I need a taskforce. What bigger change??? That would be the fulfillment of my life's "mission" to open a Nurture The Children Camp, I call it Camp Ina Maka for now, the board of directors may decide on a different name.

–What's on the horizon - where are future dreams for NTC taking you?

On the horizon: buying land and developing the back to the earth camp. There will not be a lot of construction but there will be some buildings to house the elders, offices and conference area so that the camp can rent it out to make money. All buildings will be a combination of current sustainable housing and traditional housing, all power will be produced on site (water, wind, and solar), I would like to see it stand as an example of living in harmony. While it will include some of the modern technology only earth friendly technology will be used.

The children will be housed in traditional Lakota villages; each Tipi family will have to learn to function as a family providing for their own needs. Food will be provided but they will have to prepare it, they will have to gather their wood, haul their water.

Their biggest responsibility will be to each other…the main rule will be that decisions must be made based on what is best for the "good of all". They must learn first and foremost the difference between I "want" and "need".

I want to pull them away from the reservations, cities even small towns and back to the land. Then they can go back to the reservation and share what they have learned. Ideally the youth that finish the program will be given first choice for the jobs of camp counselor for the next session should they decide to stay.

Carole Bubar-Blodgett, NTC

https://www.facebook.com/caroleblodgett/